Young Learner's

Look-n-Colour OPPOSITES, SHAPES AND COLOURS

OPPOSITES

INSIDE

OUTSIDE

HOT

COLD

SWEET

SOUR

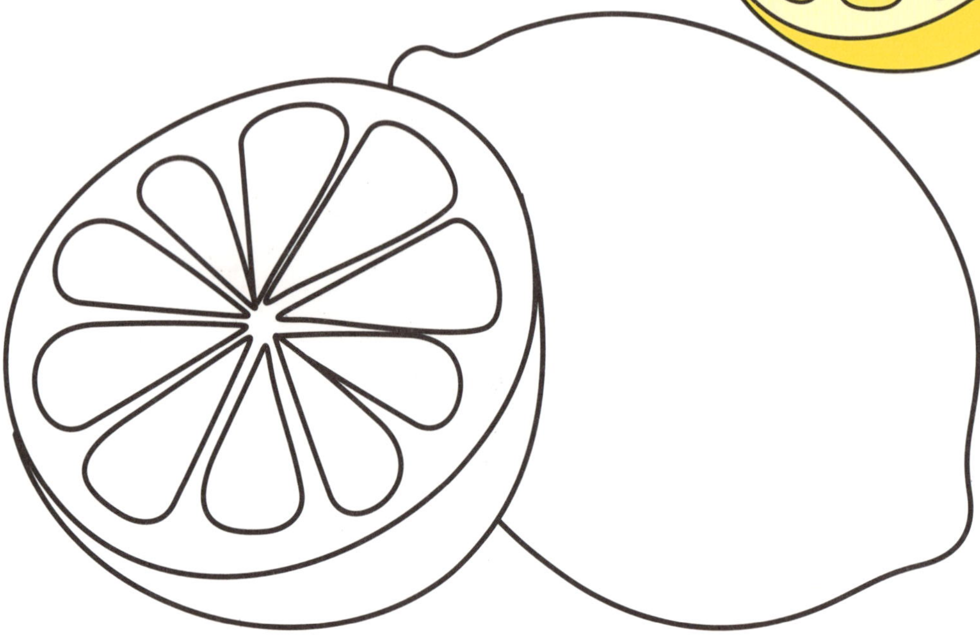

BIG

SMALL

FULL

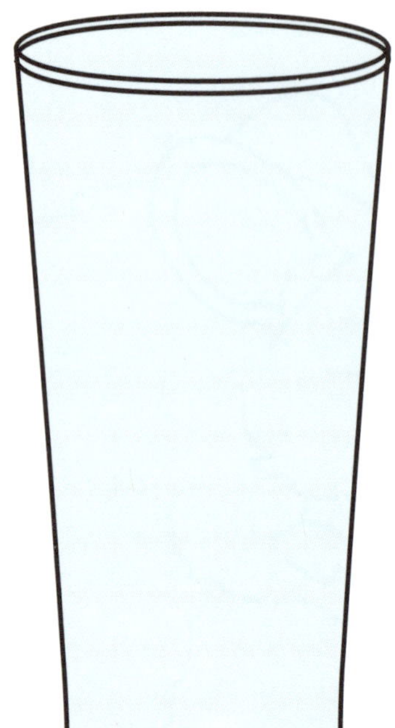

EMPTY

WET

DRY

DIRTY

CLEAN

THICK

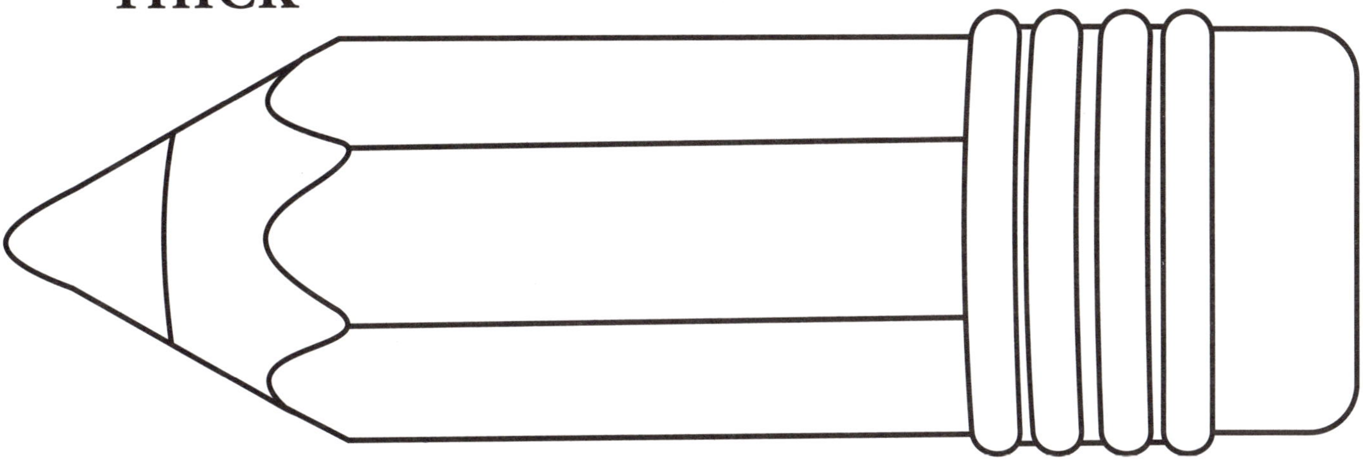

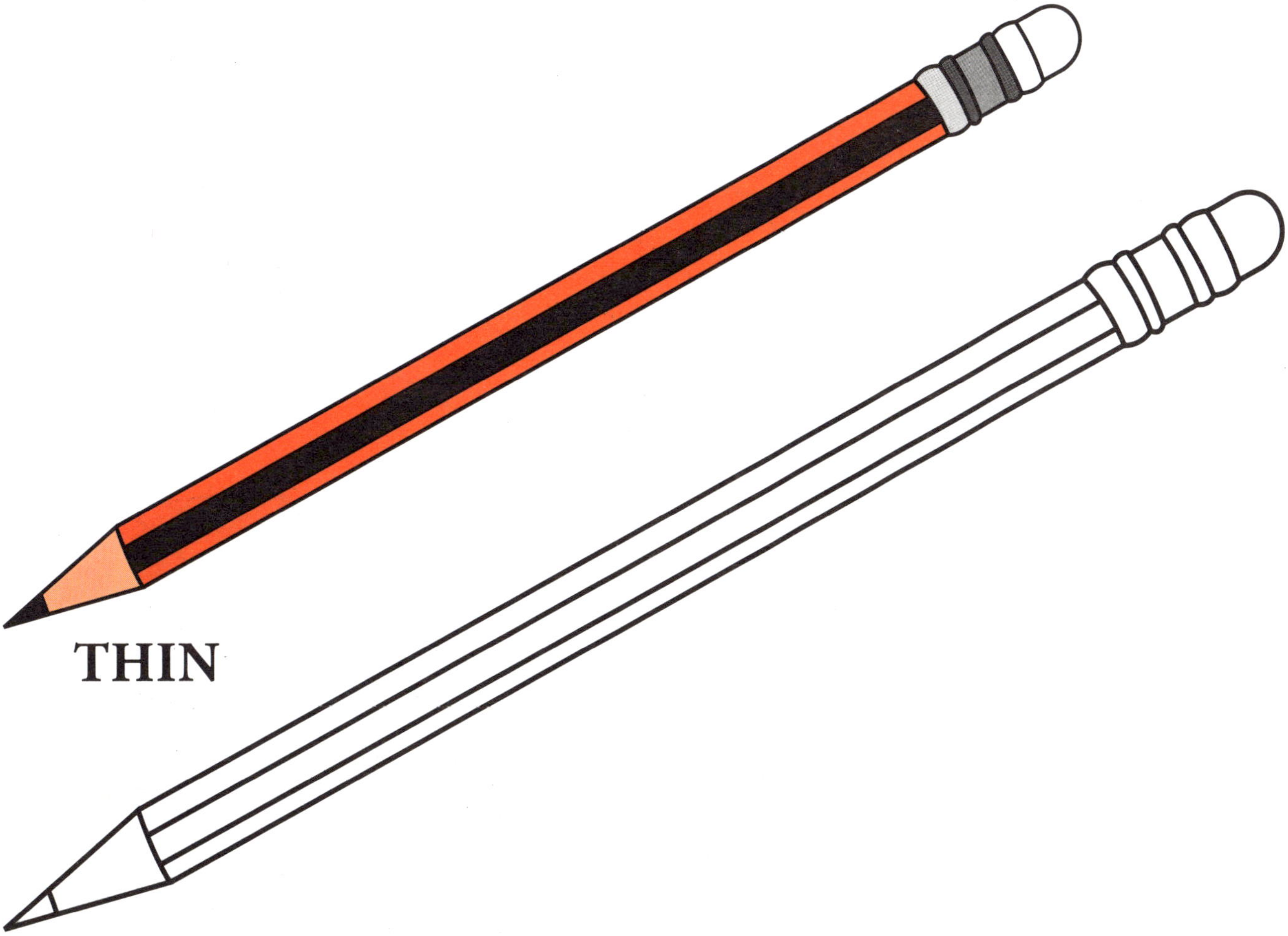

THIN

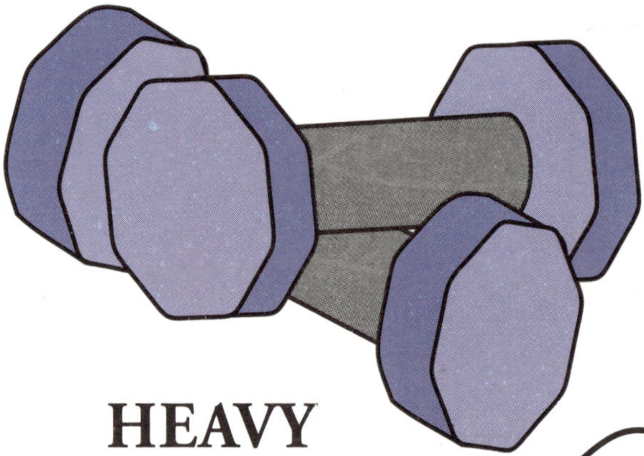

HEAVY

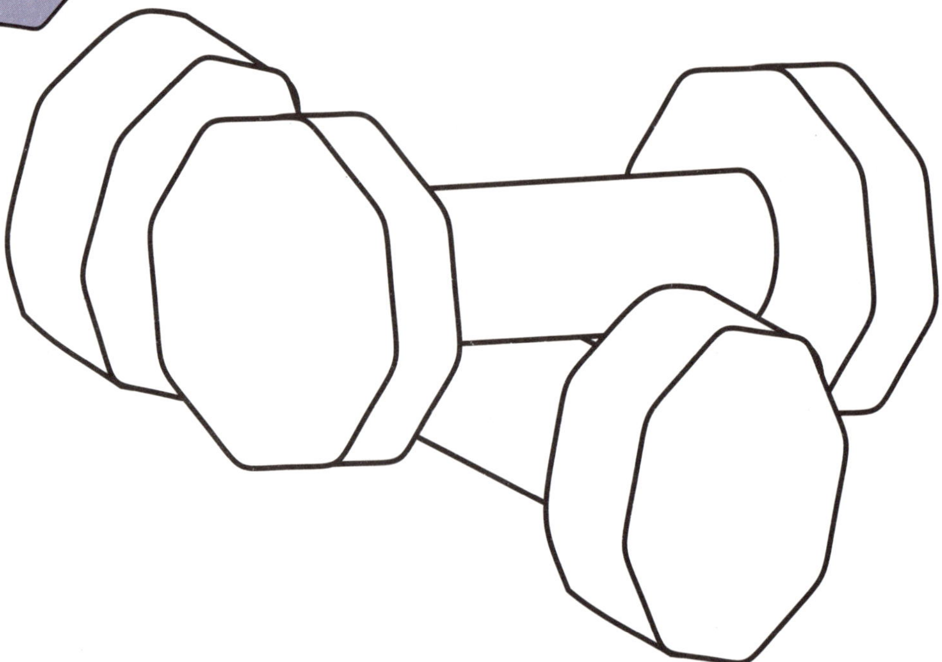

LIGHT

SHAPES

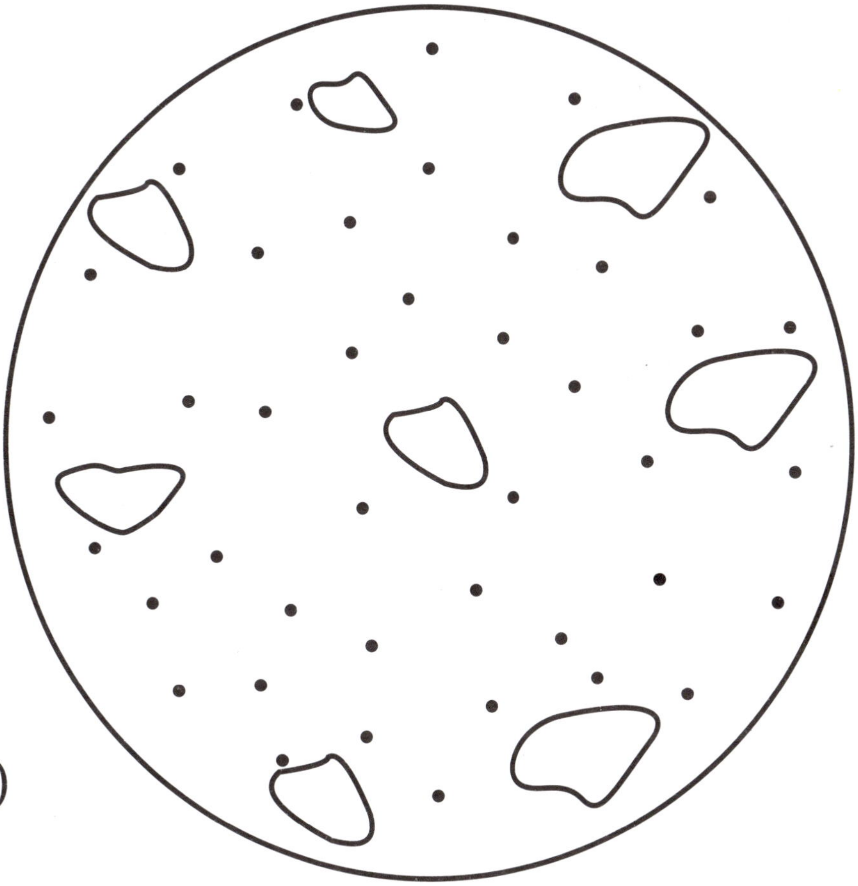

CIRCLE (COOKIE)

RECTANGLE
(WRITING BOARD)

SQUARE
(PHOTO FRAME)

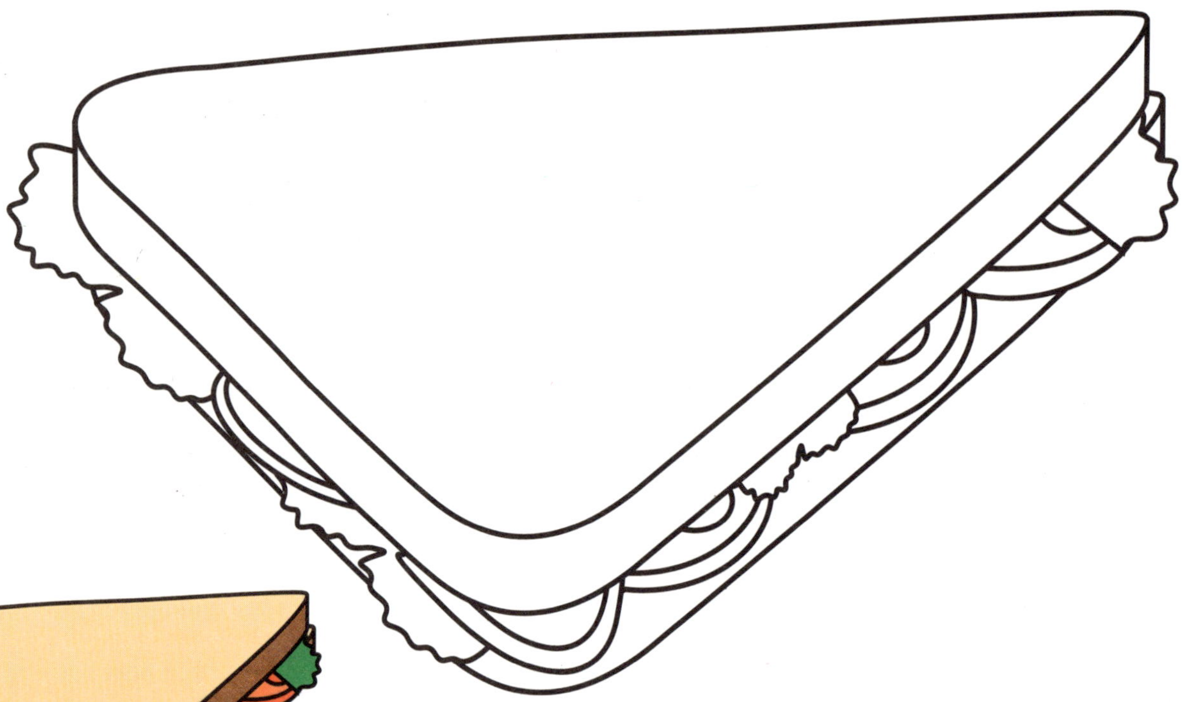

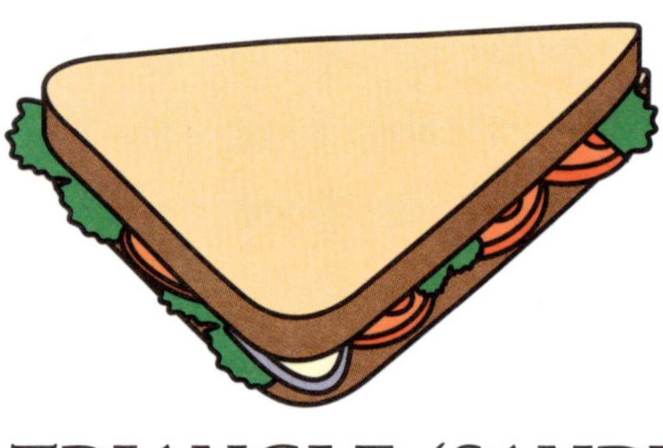

TRIANGLE (SANDWICH)

OVAL (EGG)

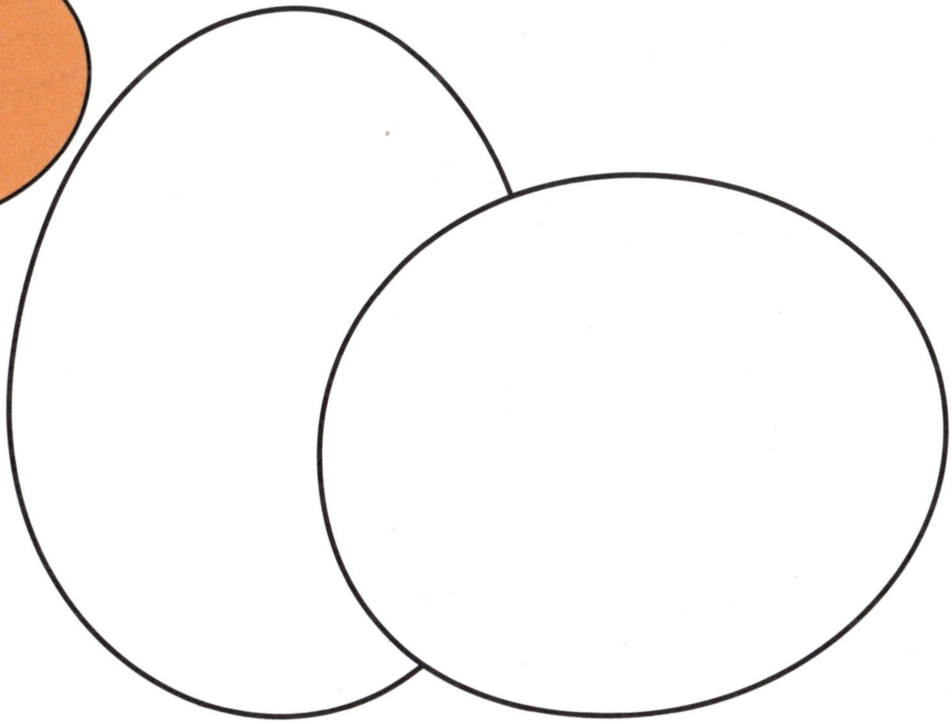

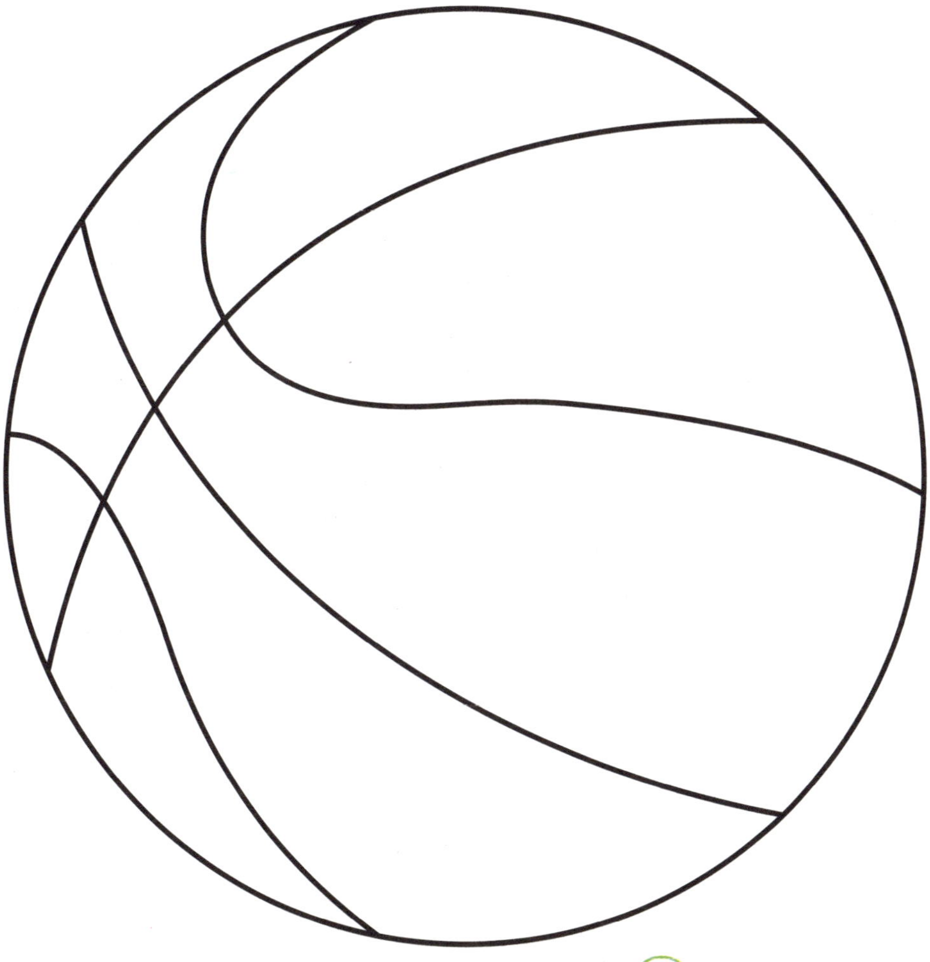

SPHERE (BASKETBALL)

CYLINDER
(SOFT DRINK CAN)

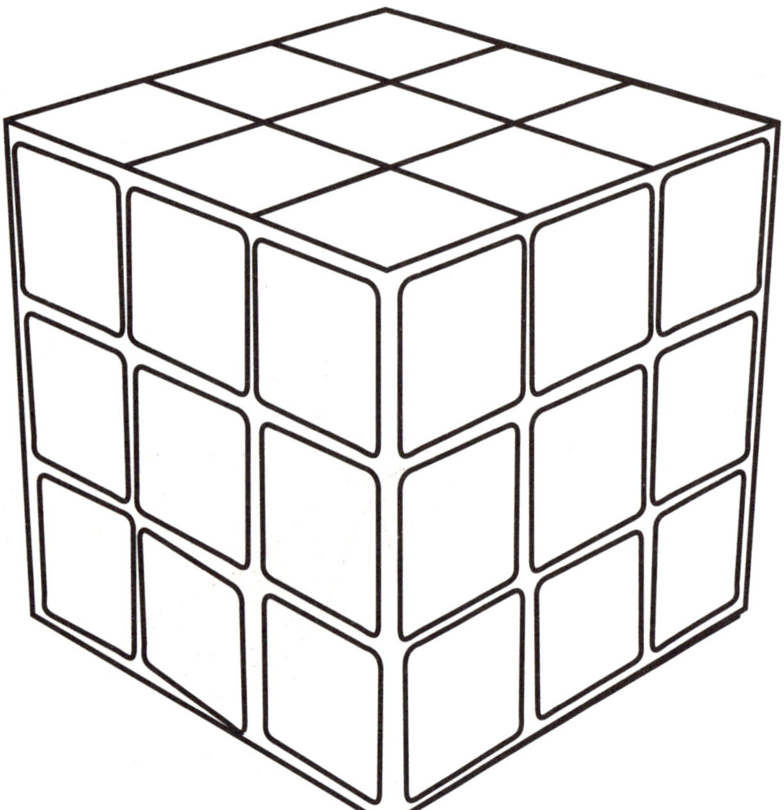

CUBE
(CUBIC PUZZLE)

HEART (BALLOON)

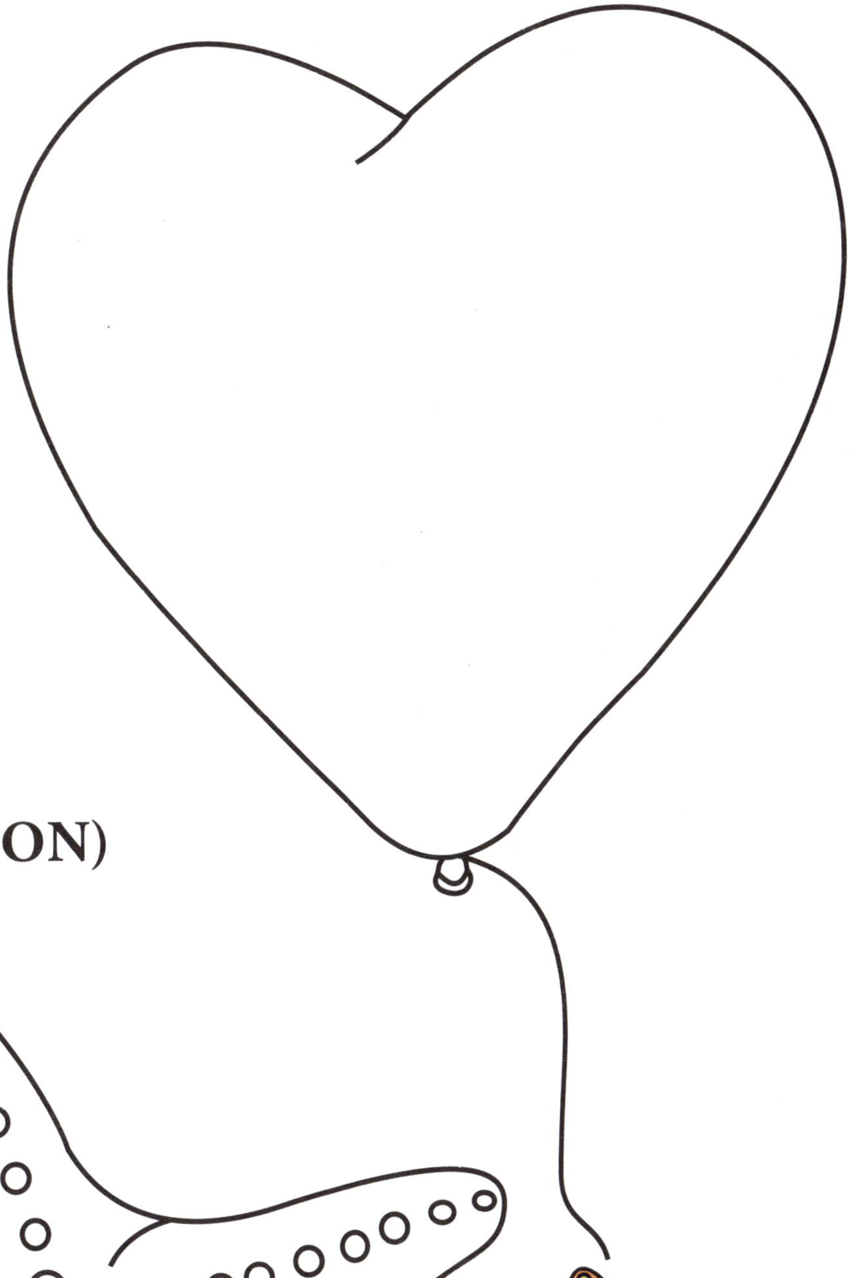

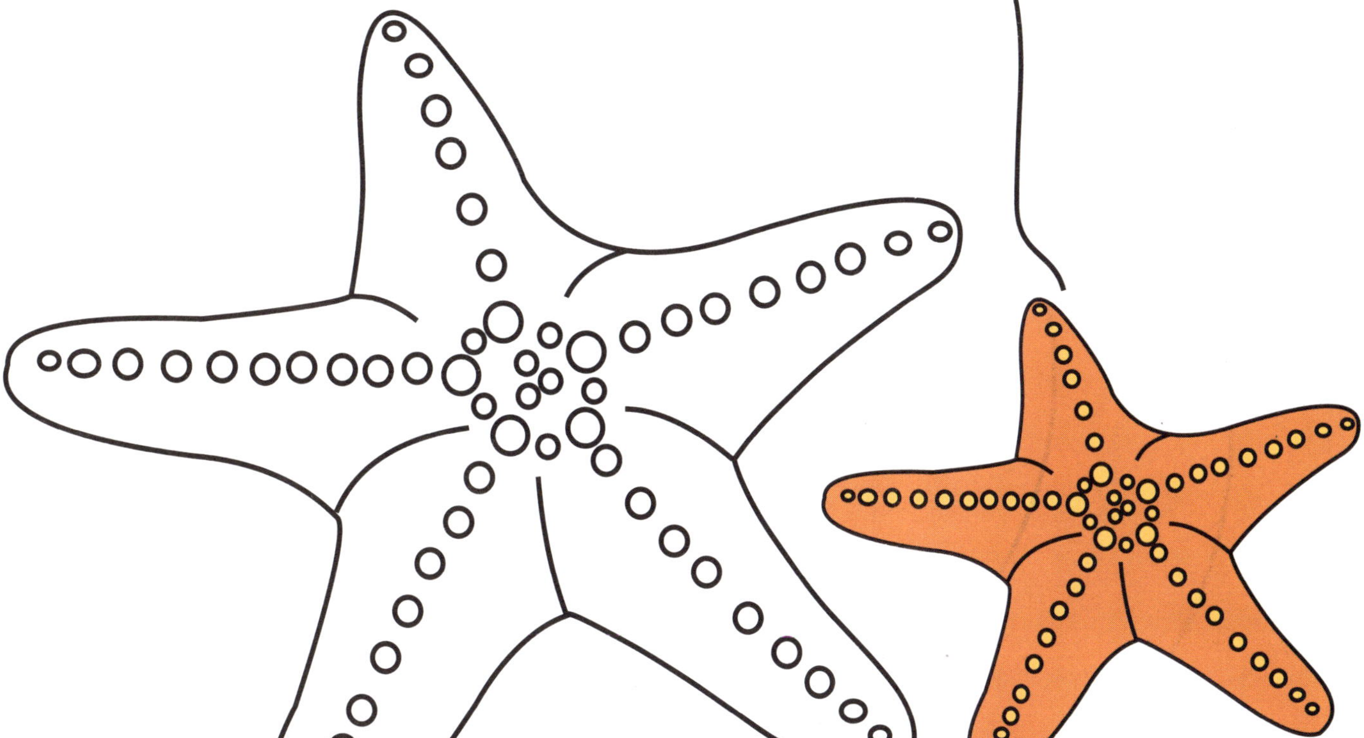

STAR (STARFISH)

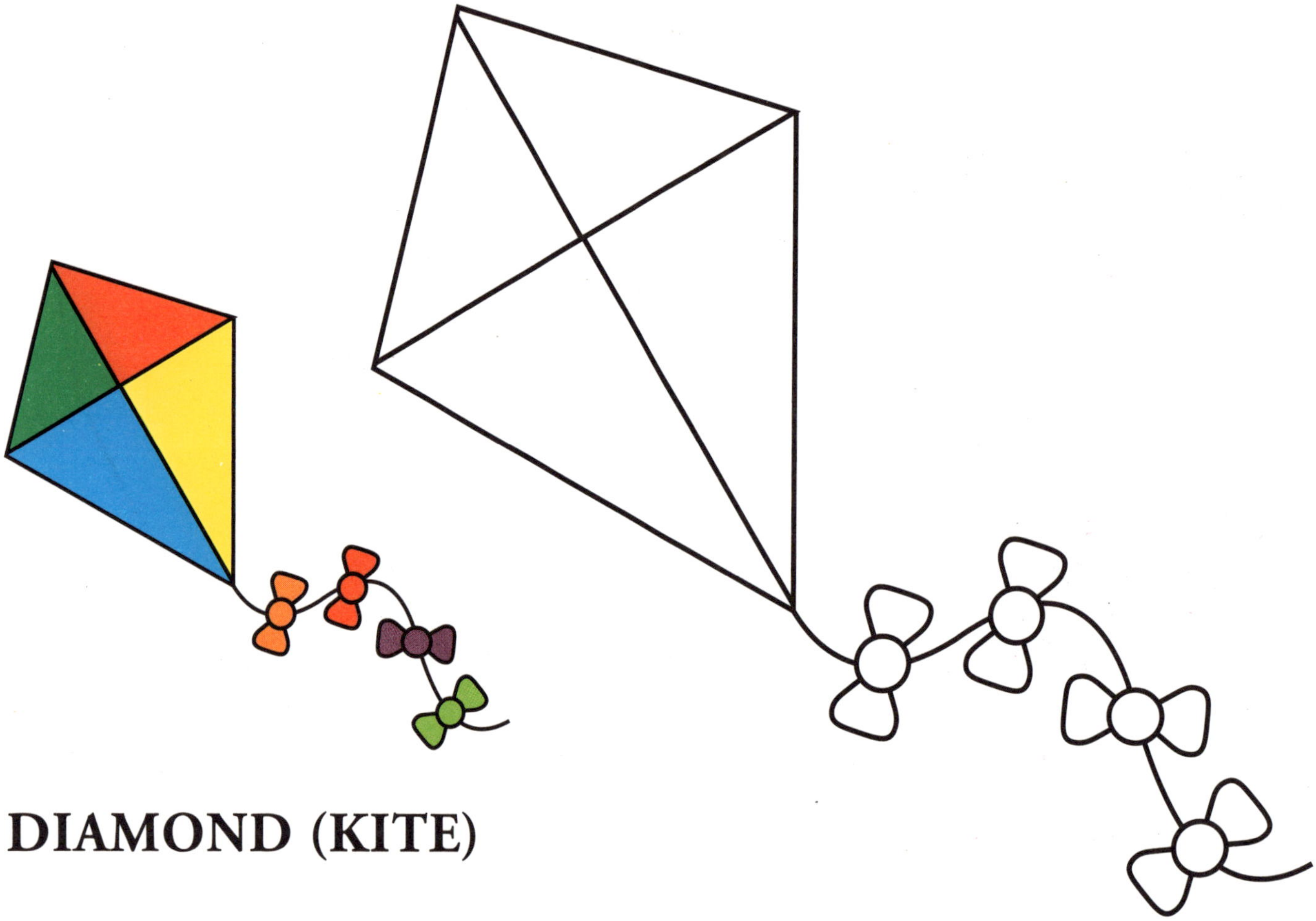

DIAMOND (KITE)

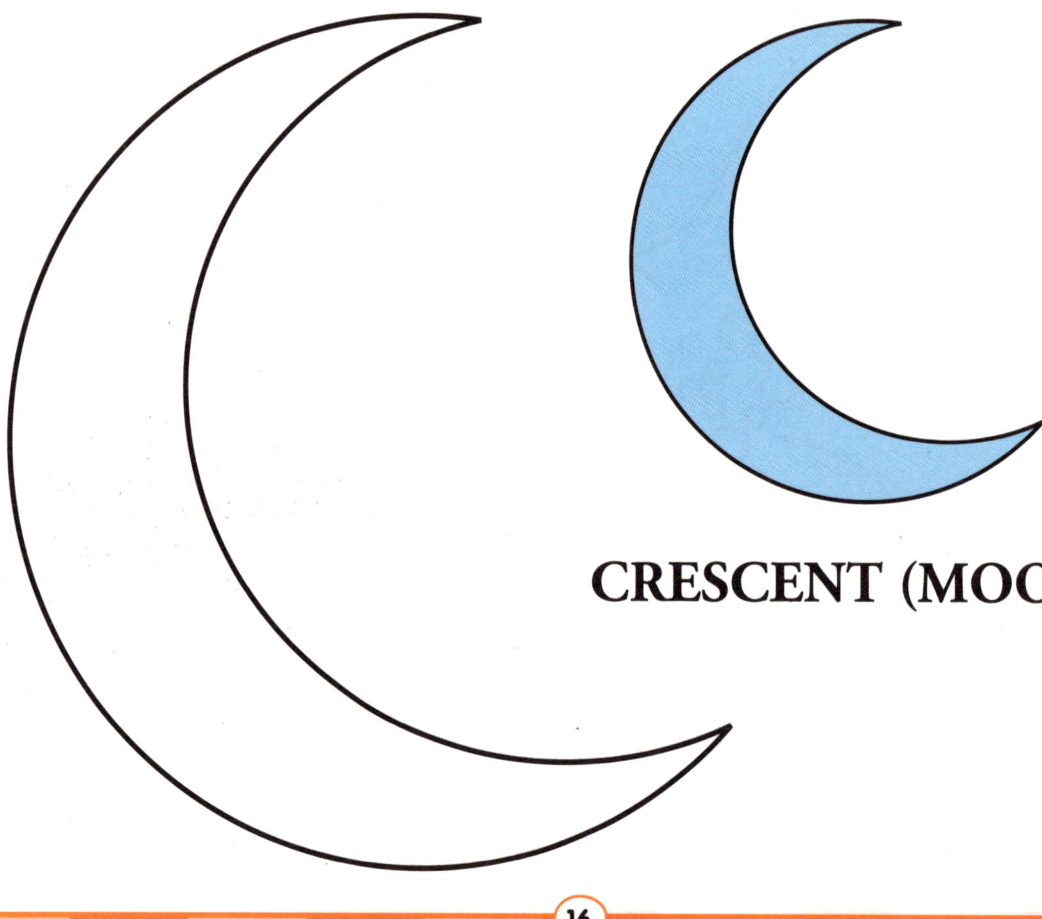

CRESCENT (MOON)

CUBOID (CUPBOARD)

CONE (BIRTHDAY CAP)

SEMICIRCLE (RAINBOW)

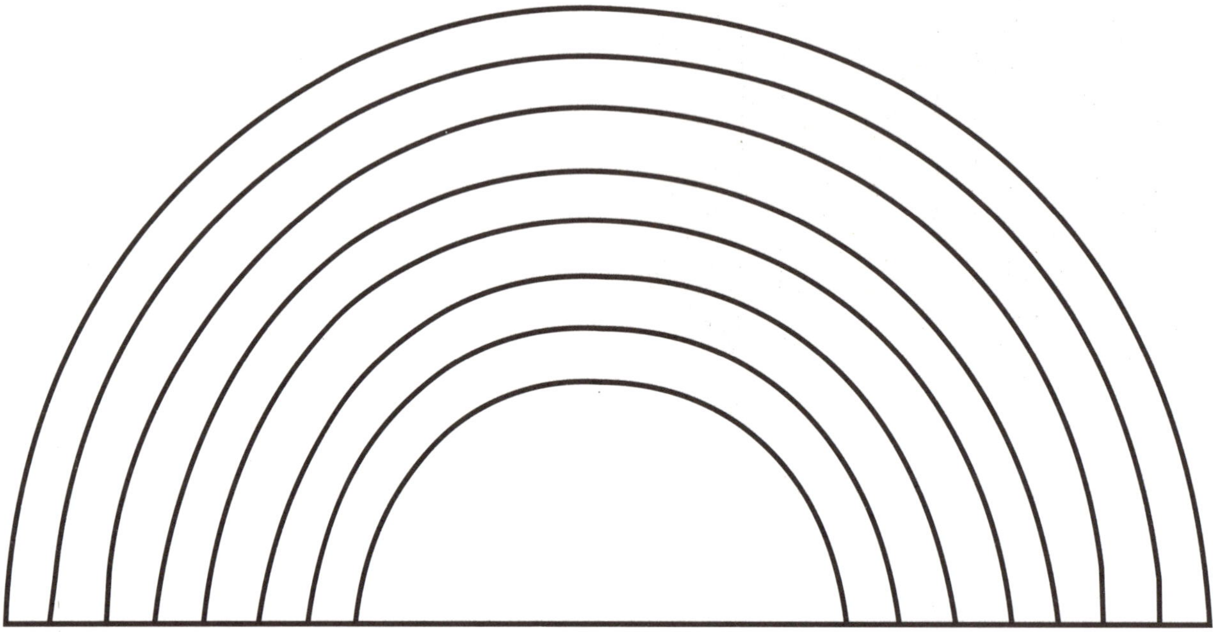

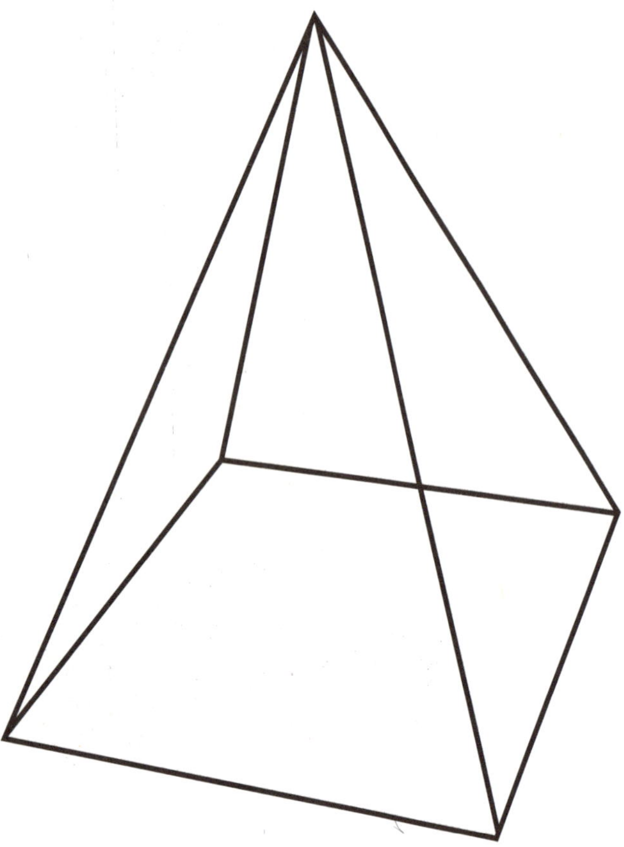

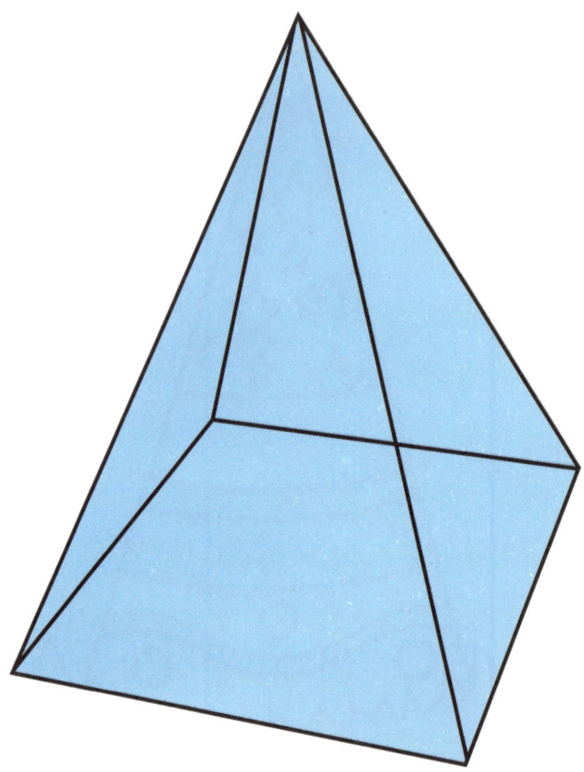

PYRAMID (PRISM)

COLOURS

RED (APPLE)

GREEN (GRAPES)

YELLOW (SUNFLOWER)

BLUE (CUP)

ORANGE (CAP)

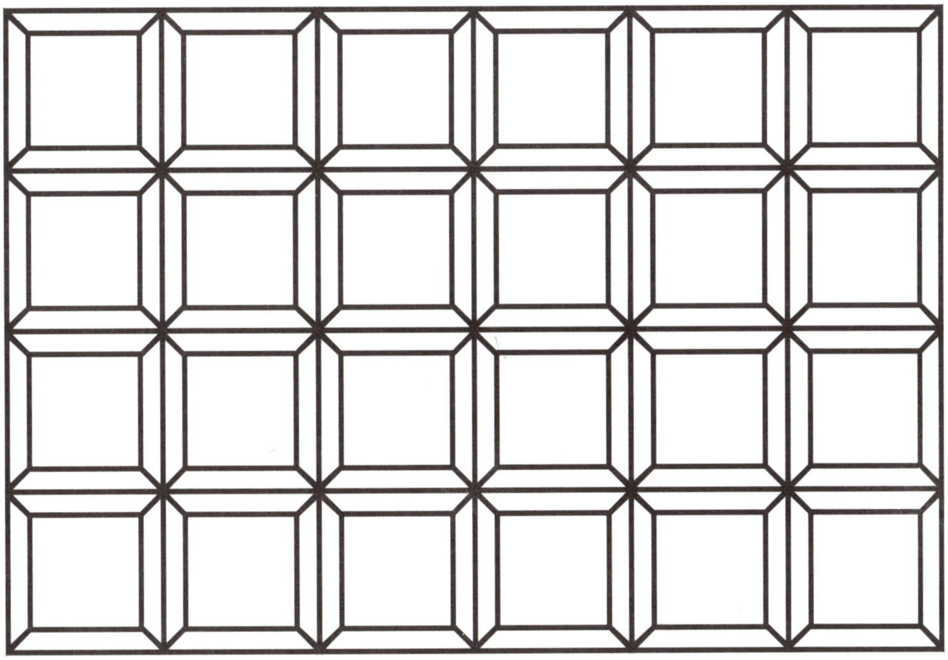

BROWN (CHOCOLATE)

PURPLE (JACKET)

PINK
(TEDDY BEAR)

BLACK (CROW)

WHITE (MILK)

MUSTARD (DRESS)

GREY (WHALE)